Finding R :
The Great
Alphabet Hunt

Paula Curtis Taylorson

illustrated by Olesya Burina

Finding R : The Great Alphabet Hunt

This is a work of fiction.

Text and Illustrations copyrighted

by Paula Curtis Taylorson ©2021

Library of Congress Control Number: 2021904826

Printed in the United States of America

A 2 Z Press LLC

PO Box 582

Deleon Springs, FL 32130

bestlittleonlinebookstore.com

sizemore3630@aol.com

440-241-3126

ISBN: 978-1-954191-19-8

Dedication

*Thank you to those
who read to me and
those who listened
to me read.*

Little **Ruby Richards** has
a **robot** made of tin.
No one **rattles** like her **rusty**
Raymond, she's so in love with him.

They sang to **reggae** on the **radio**.
They danced a **rumba** and a **reel**.

And when they cooked a **rib roast**,
it was a most **resplendent** meal!

Rambling in the bright sun's **rays**,
arm in arm the pair would go.
They **roamed** everywhere together
through the **rain** and driving snow.

But **Ruby** **roused** one morning and
her **robot** was nowhere to be found.
She **rummaged** through the **rooms** and to
the **rafters**. She just went **round** and **round**.

Why had he **run** away? He
didn't even say goodbye.
She **reached** out and called his
name, but he did not **reply**.

Had **rotten robbers ransacked** her
room and **ripped** her friend away?
But **Ruby** was **resourceful**,
and made a **resolution** that day.

ROOSTER
RACE
RAMBLE
READ
REASON
RECOVER
REACH
RAINBOW
ROCKET
RABBIT

As tears **rolled** down her **reddened**
cheeks, she **realised** what she must do.
To find her **robot**, **Raymond**,
finding **R** words was the clue.

No one meant more to her.
To **reclaim** him was her plan.
And in her **rainbow rucksack**, she
rammed her pet **rat**, Rosanne.

Raring to go, they planned a
reconnaissance to find their **robotic** friend.
In case a **random reward** was **required**
Ruby grabbed **rupees** to spend.

She **reckoned** she would need some **rivets**, some engine oil, and an old **rag**. As well as some **rope**, a **rickety ratchet**, and a **Romanian repairman's** kit bag, (just in case).

She happily and **rapidly raced** out
and **rushed** down the street in a flash.
Past the **racoons** who **relaxed** in the **rubbish**
and the **raven** who looked ill with a **rash**.

A **rhino** **rapped** on the **roof** of a porch outside a Chinese **rice** shop,

And a **Russian** Cossack
eating **rhubarb** and **raspberries**
roared at a **reindeer** bellhop.

Reading the **road** signs for clues, they met a young **ram** with some **ribbons** tied in his hair. "Have you seen a **robot roaming** this way?" **Regretfully,** the ram responded, "No, he sounds quite **rare.**"

Let's cross the **river** said **Rosanne**. We can **row** under the **ramparts** of the bridge.

If we get to the **ramshackle ranch** on the nature **reserve**, we can see the whole town from the **ridge**.

Off they went, **rambling** their way up the hill, where a **romantic reception** was **ringing**. The church bells **rang** with a **rapturous** tune played by some **reptiles** and some cockroaches singing.

A **rabbit** and a **robin** **roped** a
racehorse with a **ruby ring** on his nose,

Rick, a **Rottweiler** from **Rhode** Island, went down on his **right** knee to propose.

His **radiant** fiancée **Rita**, the **Red** setter **rushed** to answer. In **rapture**, she cried, "YES!" Without **reservations** her friends watched as she **revealed** her **ravishing** wedding dress.

The **reverend** was a **regal rooster** who **rhythmically rhymed** words with such ease. The **rest** of the crowd **responded** with cheers while eating **ratatouille, raisins,** and cheese.

Rosie climbed to the top of a **robust redwood** tree and **regarded** the sight, She **rejoiced** and **reacted** with tears of **relief** as she spotted her **robot** with delight.

They jumped into a
razzle-dazzle **racing** car,
and **rocketed** down the hill,

Where a **ragamuffin** named **Rory** was **reversing** an **RV**, which he did with **remarkable** skill.

The **recycling** centre was open. There was a **rattle** and a **rumble** of metal.

Ragged and **rough** machines were lined up, to be **reduced** to a pot or a kettle.

Ruby realised Randall the
rogue repo man had picked
up her little pal. Then **rated** and **reviewed** her
friend as scrap. "Well **rescue** him I shall!"

"Stop!" Ruby **raised** up her voice and the **reason** was perfectly clear. **Resoundingly**, she called, "He's too **riveting** for **rubbish** and I'm **reclaiming** him from here!"

Conveyors **rolled Raymond** to the crusher
as **Ruby reached** and grabbed his arm.

Reunited as the **rotating rotor** blades **receded**, her **robot** was now safe from harm.

He **returned** her **reassuring** smile, it was the **result** she needed to see. Together they **rode** off on a **rickshaw** while a **rook** sang a sweet **rhapsody**.

To recap: **Ruby** took a **risk** but **reaped**
a **remedy right** at the end,
As the **R** words **rectified** their **rift** and
reunited these two **rambunctious** friends.

The End

My Very Own 'R' Words:

_____

_____

_____

_____

_____

_____

_____

_____

_____

_____

Paula Curtis-Taylorson Lives in Marston Mortaine England. She is a full-time secondary school teacher of English and English Literature. She was amongst the first of the initial students to graduate from the Uk's first BA (Hons) Creative Writing Program at the University of Bedfordshire.

Her first love is poetry and rhyme and she works hard to inspire and teach appreciation of the subject to all age groups. Many of her students have gone on to be successful writers.

Glossary

Page 1. Ruby – a girl or woman's name
Richards – Ruby's last name here
Robot - a machine that resembles a human and does mechanical, routine tasks on command
Rattles - to give out or cause a rapid succession of short, sharp sounds
Rusty - the red or orange coating that forms on the surface of metal when exposed to air and moisture
Raymond - a boy or man's name

Page 2. Reggae a style of Jamaican popular music blending blues, calypso, and rock-'n'-roll, with a strong rhythm
Radio - a wireless unit for relaying talk and music
Rumba - a dance, Cuban in origin
Reel - a Celtic dance

Page 3. Rib roast – food made with beef
Resplendent - splendid, very nice

Page 4. Rambling - to wander around in a leisurely, aimless manner, to take a course with many turns or windings, as a stream or path.
Rays - a narrow beam of light.
Roamed - walk around without direction, wander
Rain - water that falls to the earth

Page 5. Roused - to wake up
Rummaged - to search for something by looking through contents.
Rooms - an open space in a building separated by walls or partitions from other parts
Rafters - wood to support a roof.
Round and **round** – travel or move in a circular direction

Page 6. **Runaway** – to leave where one lives
Reached out - to try to gain or request help
Reply – answer

Page 7. **Rotten** - here it means bad acting
Robbers – someone who takes things that do
not belong to them
Ransacked - to search thoroughly or vigorously
through – making a mess
Room – an area that is open where
one is able to do something in
Ripped - tear something away forcibly
Resourceful - able to deal skillfully and promptly
with new situations, difficulties, etc
Resolution – a conclusion, decided on a solution

Page 8. **Rolled** - to move along turning over and over
Reddened – the color red
Realized - to come to know something
R – a letter

Page 9. **Reclaim** - to recover lost or discarded things
Rainbow - a bow or arc of seven colors appearing
in the heavens opposite the sun and caused
by the sun's rays in drops of rain
Rucksack – a backpack
Rammed - to push something with force into something
else
Rat – a small rodent wth a long tail
Rosanne - a girl's or woman's name

Page 10. **Raring** – eagerly, anxious, enthusiastic,
ready to do something
Reconnaissance - a general examination or survey
of a region, usually followed by a detailed survey.
Remarkable - extraordinary
Robotic - operating automatically, like
a robot, move with mechanical movements

Page 10 (continued) : **Random** – no specific pattern
Reward – something given for an act completed -
money, praise, objects, trophies, in exchange
Required - something necessary
Rupees - money

Page 11. **Reckoned** - to count, compute, or calculate,
as in number or amount, to esteem or consider
Rivets - a metal pin for passing through holes in two or more plates or
pieces to hold them together, usually made with a head at one end, the
other end being hammered into a head after insertion
Rag – a small cloth a worthless piece of cloth,
especially one that is torn or worn.
Rope - a strong, thick line or cord, commonly one
composed of twisted or braided strands of hemp,
flax, or the like, or of wire or other material
Rickety - likely to fall or collapse; shaky,
feeble in the joints; tottering, old, dilapidated, or
in disrepair, irregular, as motion or action
Ratchet - a toothed bar with which a pawl engages,
a mechanism consisting of such a bar or wheel with the
pawl
Romanian – a country
Repairman - someone with skill to fix something

Page 12. **Rapidly** – to do something quickly, not slow
Raced – to move quickly
Rushed - also to move quickly
Raccoons - a small animal
Relaxed – a calm manner, slowly and with purpose
Rubbish - garbage
Raven – a black bird
Rash – an area of irritation of the skin, usually red

Page 13. **Rhino** – a large African animal with a nasal horn
Rapped - to tap on something
Roof – the covering of something else – like a home, garage, car motor
Rice shop – a shop that sells rice - food

Page 14. **Russian** Cossack - a person from the southern part of Russia forming an special group of horsemen
Rhubarb – a root vegetable grown in the ground
Raspberries - a fruit
Roared - making a large/loud noise – doing something with great energy
Reindeer – a large animal resembling a deer

Page 15. **Reading** – to to look at carefully so as to understand the meaning of something written, printed, etc. like words or music or to utter aloud or render speech of things written
Road - a long, narrow way made for traveling between two or more points; street or highway.
Ram – a farm animal, a male sheep
Ribbons - a woven strip or band of fine material, as silk or rayon, varying in width and finished off at the edges, used for ornament, tying, etc.
Roaming – walking around without a specific purpose
Regretfully - to be sorry for some actions
Responded - to reply or answer in words: *to respond briefly to a question.*
to make a return by some action as if in answer: *to respond generously to a charity drive.*
to react favorably
Rare – uncommon, only a few of, something unusual

Page 16. **River** – a small area of fresh water that flows along
Row - here - to use a paddle to move along on water
Ramparts - the supports of a bridge

Page 17. **Ramshackle** - loosely made or held together; rickety; shaky
Ranch – a large farm
Reserve - an area set aside to not change
Ridge - a long, narrow elevation of land;

Page 18. **Rambling** – to move along
Romantic – feelings the generate love and goodness
Reception – a gathering of people to celebrate an occasion – such as a wedding
Ringing – a noise
Rang - a ring that happened
Rapturous - heavenly, wonderful
Reptiles - cold- blooded creatures

Page 19. **Rabbit** – small furry animal
Robin - a bird
Roped - to use a rope to catch something
Racehorse – an animal, a horse that competes for speed
Ruby ring - a red stone ring to wear on a finger

Page 20. **Rottweiler** - a breed of dog
Rick - a boy or man's name
Rhode Island - a State in America
Right – a direction or position 'to the right'
Radiant – glowing, happy, bright,
Rita - a girl's name
Red setter – a breed of dog
Rushed - to do something quickly
Rapture - excited
Reservations – something hesitated
Revealed - to show
Ravishing - lovely

Page 21. **Reverend** – a minister
Regal - pertaining to royalty
Rooster - a farm bird that cock-a-doodle-doos
Rhythmically - with a steady beat
Rhymed - common sound of words of verse.
Rest – relaxed and stop working
Responded - say or do something in reply
Ratatouille – food consisting of eggplant, zucchini, onions,
green peppers, tomatoes, and garlic, served hot or cold
Raisins - dried grapes, food
Robust - strong and healthy; hardy; vigorous

Page 22. **Robust** - large, stunning
Redwood – a tree
Regarded – to take notice of one's likes or preferences
Rejoiced - something to be happy about, thankful for
Reacted - to act in response to an agent or influence
Relief - alleviation, ease, or deliverance through the
removal of pain or distress

Page 23. **Razzle** - fancy
Racing car – **a car to be fast**
Rocketed - to move like a rocket, fast
(of game birds) to fly straight up rapidly when flushed

Page 24. **Ragamuffin** - a type of cat (here)
Rory - a boy's name
Reversing – going backwards
RV – abbreviation for recreational
vehicle – a vehicle one travels and sleeps in
Remarkable - extraordinarily good

Page 25. **Recycling** – to make useful use again
after being used
Rattle - to cause a rapid succession of
short, sharp sounds,
Rumble - a deep, heavy, somewhat muffled sound

Page 26. **Ragged** - not in the best condition
Rough - not in the best condition
Reduced – to make smaller

Page 27. **Realized** - to be aware when once were not
Randall - a boy or man's name
Rogue - a scoundrel, a playfully mischievous person
Repo man – a person who takes objects back
Rated – judge by quality
Reviewed – to look things over and evaluate
Rescue - to save from harm or loneliness

Page 28. **Raised** – to bring to the attention
of someone –to elevate something
Reason - a basis for some fact
Resoundingly - uttered loudly
Riveting - stunning
Rubbish - garbage
Reclaiming - take back

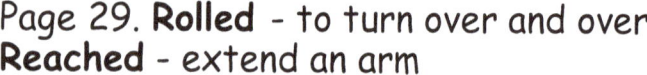

Page 29. **Rolled** - to turn over and over
Reached - extend an arm

Page 30. **Reunited** – to bring together again
Rotating - moving in a circular motion
Rotor - a unit used to make a machine work
Receded – to draw or pull backwards

Page 31. **Returned** – to give something or get something back
Reassuring - to remove doubt and fear
Result - the outcome.
Rode - to sit on something and carried away
Rickshaw - a small, two-wheeled, cart-like passenger
vehicle with a fold-down top, pulled by one person
Rook - a black, European crow
Rhapsody - very happy

Page 32. **Recap** - to give a brief summary of events

Risk - exposure to the chance of injury or loss;

Reaped - to receive a reward or result that is due to one's action

Remedy - a result

Right – correct

Rectified – make something right and good that was hurt or damaged or lost

Rift - a conflict or argument between parties – difference of opinion

Reunited - to bring together again

Rambunctious - difficult to control or handle

www.ingramcontent.com/pod-product-compliance
Lightning Source LLC
Chambersburg PA
CBHW041126120626
46547CB00019B/2877